Cardiff.Mum's
Thrifty Feasts

Deliciously affordable **one-pan**, **air-fryer** and **slow-cooker** meals for every home and budget

MICHAEL JOSEPH

I want to dedicate this book first to my parents, Tony and Carol, for the days and nights you've looked after my children so that I could put the time into these recipes, but also to my AMAZING followers. I feel like you are my friends and without you this book wouldn't have been possible. I really hope you and everyone in your house loves these recipes and that the book helps you to save money and enjoy food shopping and cooking. I can't wait to see you re-create them!

Cardiff.Mum's
Thrifty Feasts

Ashleigh Mogford

Photography by Ella Miller

Contents

Welcome!

Hey Lovelies!

First off, thank you so much for purchasing Thrifty Feasts. I am beyond proud of it! I've wanted to give you a book full of feel-good family recipes like the ones from my Instagram page for so long. I love making food videos but nothing beats a written-down recipe, so I'm thrilled that I can finally share them here in book form. My vision when writing this book was for it to be a staple item in your (and my!) kitchen, one that is used weekly to help you plan your food shops and make utterly delicious feasts, while hopefully saving you a few much-needed pennies in the process. Knowing that you're now holding it in your hands and will hopefully use it in that way brings me so much joy!

I started sharing recipes on my Cardiff.mum Instagram page back in the summer of 2020, when I was on maternity leave with my first daughter, Addie. I was loving every minute of being a mum, but was struggling to survive on statutory maternity pay. I was looking for ways to stretch my budget and was keen to share them with my followers. If you followed me from the beginning, you'll know that initially a large chunk of my content focused on our daily adventures and ideas for fun family days out; but these things all cost money and I soon learned a few tricks to help me budget with things like the weekly food shop, to help keep a bit back to spend on the fun stuff! I've always loved cooking, and we love feel-good, flavour-packed food in my house, so I was never going to pull back on the quality of meals. Budget food can often feel drab, but I wanted to find a way to save some money and still cook vibrant meals that were really delicious and celebratory. To do this I just planned well, shopped better and cooked clever. I started showing other people how you can still make really good food if you're savvy with your food shopping, and the content took off, with millions of views, newspaper articles and radio interviews over just a few months, which is how Cardiff.mum became so popular. It was a whirlwind, but I am so grateful for the journey and where it has taken me!

I will say, I'm not a trained chef by any means. I've never had to write recipes down before and I have no professional background in cooking – I'm actually trained as a geography teacher and love to travel, so perhaps that's why I've always been adventurous with trying new flavours and cuisines, looking to bring them into my own home cooking. I love adding smart twists to comforting favourites and creating meals with exciting flavours and textures. I just love food that makes you feel good! Since becoming a mum, I'm also really passionate about people saving money so that they can do more things that they love, and I really hope this book helps you to do that.

To help make the meals as economical as possible, the ingredients that I use throughout my recipes are cheap, versatile, accessible and can be purchased from budget supermarkets. In these pages I will show you techniques to easily add wonderful flavours to your dishes that don't involve having to buy lots of expensive ingredients. I'm a huge believer that the store cupboard is your best friend, and every recipe in this book has ingredients that can be shared across several other meals, meaning that if you plan well and shop smart you can use the same ingredients again and again, but still have meals that feel fresh and new every time. (For more information on my must-have store cupboard items, see page 14.)

I hope that you enjoy the Thrifty Feasts in these pages as much as I and my family do. I'd love to see the results, so do tag me in anything that you make. Happy cooking!

Ash x

£5-and-Under
Feasts

Creamy Garlic Mushroom Risotto

SERVES: 4 • TIME: 30 MINUTES

In my opinion, a creamy garlic mushroom risotto is a restaurant-quality dish, rich, velvety and flavoursome. I like to serve it sloppy and mop up the creamy, garlic sauce with warm bread. Such a comforting, moreish family dinner.

1. Finely chop the garlic, onion and celery. Defrost the mushrooms and spinach, if using frozen, using the microwave. Drain the mushrooms but keep the liquid. Place the mushroom liquid in a jug with a veg stock cube and top it up to 850ml with hot water.

2. Put the mushrooms into a pan with 1 tablespoon of butter, the thyme and the chopped garlic and cook until the mushrooms are golden. When cooked, remove them from the pan. Finely chop half the mushrooms.

3. Add the chopped onion and celery to the same pan and cook for a few minutes, until soft.

4. Add the risotto rice to the pan and stir for 2 minutes to toast and combine well with the vegetables.

5. Slowly start adding the stock. Add a ladle at a time, stirring the risotto after each one, and don't add any more until the previous ladle of stock has evaporated.

6. Continue to add stock until your rice is nearly cooked. Then add the chopped mushrooms and spinach, and keep adding stock until the rice is tender.

7. Chop the parsley. Stir 1 tablespoon of cream cheese and 1 tablespoon of butter into the rice, then add the grated Cheddar, season with salt and pepper and finish with the rest of the mushrooms and chopped parsley.

4 cloves of garlic

1 large onion

2 celery sticks

500g frozen mushrooms

100g frozen or fresh spinach

1 veg stock cube

2 tablespoons butter

1 teaspoon dried thyme

300g risotto rice

a handful of fresh parsley

1 tablespoon cream cheese

100g grated Cheddar cheese

salt and pepper

Stovetop Minestrone Soup + Cheesy Croutons

SERVES: 4 • TIME: 40 MINUTES

I nearly called this 'never throw out your leftover veg or bread soup'. I make it once a month with all the odd ends of veg and a bit of stale bread and it goes down a treat. There's nothing more comforting or nourishing, and the cheese-topped croutons make it that extra bit special.

1. Chop the onion, carrots, celery, red pepper and garlic, and put them into a large soup pan with a few tablespoons of olive oil. Cook over a medium heat, and when they have softened, add the stock and cook for 10 minutes more.

2. Drain the cannellini beans and sweetcorn and add them to the pan, then add the pasta and cook for another 15 minutes.

3. Preheat the oven to 200°C fan. Chop the bread into small squares, put them on a baking tray, drizzle with oil, season with salt and pepper, and place in the oven for 5 minutes.

4. Remove the tray from the oven and sprinkle half the grated cheese over the croutons, then place under a hot grill for 5 minutes to melt the cheese.

5. Finely chop the basil and parsley and add to the soup. Stir in the red pesto and cook for 5 more minutes.

6. Serve in bowls, with the Cheddar croutons and the rest of the grated cheese sprinkled on top.

1 red onion

2 carrots

3 celery sticks

1 red pepper

3 cloves of garlic

olive oil

2 litres chicken or veg stock

1 x 400g tin of cannellini beans

1 x 150g tin of sweetcorn

400g fusilli pasta

4 slices of stale bread

salt and pepper

200g grated Cheddar cheese

a handful of fresh basil

a handful of fresh parsley

3 tablespoons red pesto

Harissa Chicken Couscous Bowl

SERVES: 4 • TIME: 40 MINUTES

This is a favourite among my followers. I make it often, because I love the textures of slow-cooked chicken with fluffy couscous. Harissa seasoning is the perfect spice for it – it's fragrant, fruity and smoky, and goes so well with chicken. A real winner.

1. Slice the chicken thighs and place them in a bowl. Grate the garlic and add to the bowl with 1 tablespoon of Greek yoghurt and 1 tablespoon of harissa seasoning. Season with salt and pepper, mix well, then cover and pop into the fridge to marinate for a few hours.

2. When ready to cook, preheat the oven to 200°C fan. Put the chicken into a frying pan with 1 tablespoon of olive oil and cook for 3–4 minutes on each side or, until cooked through.

3. Meanwhile, put the couscous into a bowl with some salt and pepper and the amount of boiling water stated on the packet. Cover for 10 minutes, until the water has been absorbed.

4. Drain the chickpeas and put them on a baking tray. Drizzle with 1 tablespoon of olive oil and season with salt and pepper, sprinkle with 1 tablespoon of harissa seasoning, and bake in the oven for 10 minutes, until golden.

5. Chop the cucumber and add it to the couscous. Cut the lemon in half, then squeeze one half over the couscous and mix everything together.

6. Put the remaining yoghurt into a little plastic sandwich bag or something similar, and mix in the juice of the remaining half lemon and the chopped mint. Cut off a tiny corner of the bag to create a hole so that you can drizzle the yoghurt mixture.

7. Chop the red onion. Layer your chicken on top of the couscous, with the roasted chickpeas and the chopped red onion, then drizzle the yoghurt mixture over the top.

8. Top with a sprinkle of chilli flakes.

600g chicken thighs
3 cloves of garlic
3 heaped tablespoons, Greek yoghurt
2 tablespoons harissa seasoning
salt and pepper
2 tablespoons olive oil
2 packets/200g lemon and coriander flavoured couscous
1 x 400g tin of chickpeas
½ a cucumber
1 lemon
a handful of fresh mint, chopped
1 small red onion
1 teaspoon chilli flakes

SPRUCE IT UP!

To dress this up (and stretch the budget slightly), mix a handful each of chopped fresh coriander and mint through the couscous, and crumble 100g of feta cheese over the dish before serving.

Lemon Ricotta Linguine

SERVES: 4 • TIME: 15 MINUTES

I love this zesty lemon ricotta linguine. It's perfect for your carb cravings and makes a properly delish weeknight meal that is ready in less than 15 minutes. Simple, fresh ingredients, delicious flavour and minimal effort.

1. Cook your pasta in a large pan of salted boiling water until al dente (nearly cooked).

2. Chop the garlic and the baby spinach. Put the ricotta, Parmesan, garlic, lemon juice and a little zest into a bowl with plenty of salt and pepper, and mix.

3. Scoop out a cup of cooking water from the pan, then drain the pasta.

4. Put the drained pasta back into the pan and add your ricotta mix and the chopped spinach. Stir in about 150ml of the pasta cooking water.

5. Serve in bowls, with wedges of lemon, and grate over a little more zest.

320g linguine
2 cloves of garlic
250g fresh or defrosted frozen baby spinach
250g ricotta
50g Parmesan cheese
zest and juice of 1 lemon
salt and pepper
4 lemon wedges, to serve

Creamy Harissa Pasta + Cod

SERVES: 4 • TIME: 30 MINUTES

Pasta is my go-to budget meal. Adding harissa to a tomatoey sauce gives it a tangy, spicy kick, but the cream tones it down and adds a buttery richness to the dish. It's smoky, rich and every spoonful has a burst of flavour.

1. Preheat the oven to 200°C on the grill setting.

2. Cook your pasta in salted boiling water according to the instructions on the packet. Add the kale to the water for the final two minutes of cooking. Drain and reserve a ladle of pasta water.

3. Drizzle the cod fillets with 1 tablespoon of olive oil, the lemon juice, salt and pepper, and spoon/sprinkle over the harissa. Air fry for 7 minutes at 190°C.

4. Chop the garlic, then place it in a blender with the mascarpone, Parmesan and sun-dried tomatoes and blitz until smooth.

5. Put the pasta and kale back into the pan, and add the creamy sauce mixture and the reserved pasta water.

6. Mix well, adding the parsley and serve.

400g spaghetti

100g sliced kale

4 small frozen cod fillets, defrosted

1 tablespoon olive oil

juice of half a lemon

salt and pepper

1 tablespoon harissa seasoning or paste

2 cloves of garlic

250g mascarpone

50g Parmesan cheese

200g sun-dried tomatoes

chopped parsley, to serve

Halloumi Coconut Curry

SERVES: 4 • TIME: 30 MINUTES

I was always scared of cheese in a curry, until recently, when I ordered a takeaway and they sent me a paneer curry by mistake. I ate it and couldn't stop thinking about it for days, so of course I had to recreate it, but using my fave – halloumi. The crispy cheese and creamy coconutty curry sauce together are . . . dreamy.

1. Slice the red pepper and onion, and chop the garlic. Put them into a pan with the soy sauce and ginger purée and fry in a little oil until they start to soften.

2. Add the Thai red curry paste, peanut butter and coconut milk, and stir together.

3. Cut the halloumi into 12 slices. In a separate pan, fry them in a little oil until golden and crispy, then add them to the curry sauce.

4. Serve the curry over rice.

1 red pepper

1 onion

3 cloves of garlic

2 tablespoons soy sauce

1 tablespoon ginger purée

olive oil

2 tablespoons Thai red curry paste

1 tablespoon peanut butter

1 x 400ml tin of full fat coconut milk

1 packet of halloumi (225–250g)

To serve
cooked jasmine rice

SPRUCE IT UP!

To dress this up (and stretch the budget slightly), scatter some chopped roasted peanuts and fresh chopped coriander over the dish before serving.

Garlic Butter Lemon Prawn Linguine

SERVES: 4 • TIME: 45 MINUTES

I always stock up on frozen prawns for making this dish. It's just a super-speedy, delicious midweek meal. Prawns go best with lemon and garlic, in my opinion.

1. Defrost your prawns under cold running water, then drain and pat them dry. Chop the garlic and parsley.

2. Put the prawns into a bowl with half the garlic, half the parsley, the juice of half the lemon, 3 tablespoons of butter and a pinch of chilli flakes. Add plenty of salt and pepper, mix, then cover and leave in the fridge for 30 minutes.

3. Cook your pasta in salted boiling water according to the instructions on the packet. When it's ready, drain, reserving 100ml of the cooking water.

4. Finely chop the onion and fry it in a frying pan with the rest of the chopped garlic and a drizzle of oil until softened. Stir in the wine, if using, bring to the boil and simmer for 2 minutes to reduce, then add your prawns and their marinade and fry for a few minutes until they are all pink.

5. Stir in the pasta and the reserved cooking water. Add the Parmesan and the juice of the remaining lemon half. Season with salt and pepper and serve with rocket, chilli flakes and the rest of the chopped parsley.

400g frozen prawns

4 cloves of garlic

a handful of fresh parsley

juice of 1 lemon

4 tablespoons butter

½ teaspoon chilli flakes

salt and pepper

olive oil

320g linguine or spaghetti

1 onion

150ml dry white wine (optional)

75g grated Parmesan

SPRUCE IT UP!

To dress this up (and stretch the budget slightly), drizzle 100g of asparagus tips in a little oil, spread on a baking tray and bake at 200°C fan for 10–12 minutes, until tender, then toss through the pasta along with a handful of rocket leaves and a sprinkling of chilli flakes before serving.

Sticky Mushroom Tacos

SERVES: 4 • TIME: 30 MINUTES

My friend introduced me to these after a day of drinking at Brighton Pride one summer. She whipped up the mushroom filling in a pan, handed me a spoon and a pile of flour tortillas, and we stood over the sink ramming them into our mouths, with the sauce dripping down our hands. I still say to this day that they were one of the best things I've ever eaten.

1. Chop the onion and garlic, and slice the mushrooms. Heat a little oil in a frying pan and add the onion, garlic and the ginger purée. Fry for a few minutes, until the onion starts to soften, then add the mushrooms and cook for 5 minutes.

2. Add the garam masala and soy sauce and cook for another 5 minutes, until the liquid has been absorbed and the mushrooms are soft. Add the honey and a pinch of chilli flakes and cook for another 2 minutes, then transfer to a bowl.

3. Heat your tortillas on the open flame of the hob or in a hot frying pan, and serve in bowls for people to load them up with mushrooms and fresh mint leaves.

1 small white onion
1 clove of garlic
500g mixed mushrooms
2 tablespoons olive oil
1 teaspoon ginger purée
2 teaspoons garam masala
3 tablespoons dark soy sauce
3 tablespoons honey
chilli flakes
8 small flour tortillas
a handful of fresh mint leaves

SPRUCE IT UP!

To dress this up (and stretch the budget slightly), make a quick mint slaw by finely chopping half a small red cabbage, 1 red onion, quarter of an iceberg lettuce and a handful of fresh mint leaves, then combine in a bowl with 3 tablespoons of mayonnaise, the juice of 1 lemon and a pinch of salt.

Deep Pan Pizzas

SERVES: 4 • TIME: 40 MINUTES

You could order a Domino's. Or you could whip up some deep pan pizzas for less than £5. I added crispy pancetta, as it's my favourite pizza topping, but you can add whichever ones you like. These are super crispy on the outside and doughy on the inside. I like to freeze a few portions of the dough for when we fancy a treat.

1. Chop the garlic and finely chop the red pepper. Fry them in a little oil for around 10 minutes, until the pepper is soft, then add the tomato purée and tinned tomatoes and cook for 5 minutes. Using a hand blender or a normal blender, blitz the sauce to make it smooth. It's fine if you don't have a blender, the sauce will just be chunky.

2. Chop the red onions and pancetta and pan fry them with the oregano in another pan. When the pancetta is crispy, remove and set aside.

3. Preheat your oven to 190°C fan.

4. Place the flour in a bowl with 100ml of water and a pinch of salt. Mix with your hands, then knead until you get a spongy dough. If the dough looks dry then add a splash more water.

5. Sprinkle some flour on a work surface and roll the dough into a round just larger than your pan.

6. Dust a large ovenproof frying pan with flour and add your rolled dough, pushing the edges into the sides of the pan to cover the base.

7. Spoon half of the sauce into the base of the pan. Add half of the pancetta and onions and half of the cheese. Then repeat with the remaining sauce, onions, pancetta and finally scatter over the remaining cheese. Place the pan on the hob over a medium to low heat for 5 minutes.

8. Put your pizza, still in the pan, into the oven for 15 minutes, or until the dough is cooked and the cheese melted and bubbling. Cool for 5 minutes then serve.

4 cloves of garlic

2 red peppers

1 tablespoon olive oil

4 tablespoons tomato purée

2 x 400g tins of plum tomatoes

2 red onions

85g smoked pancetta

½ teaspoon dried oregano

250g self-raising flour

salt

100g grated Cheddar cheese

Easy Freezy 2-Ingredient Dough

This dough is super simple to make, keeps brilliantly in the freezer and is really adaptable, making it a great fallback for when you're struggling for inspiration! Stock up your freezer with portions of the dough, and use the recipes below to liven up your midweek meals.

MAKES 8 FREEZABLE PORTIONS

250g full fat plain Greek yoghurt
400g self-raising flour

1. Put the ingredients into a large bowl and combine with a wooden spoon until smooth.

2. Use your hands to give it a final knead, to make sure the dough is super smooth. When it's ready, the dough shouldn't stick to your hands.

To use the 2-ingredient dough (each recipe is for 1 person unless it says otherwise):

Air-fryer calzones

These calzones are a great midweek meal and can be filled with anything you like. I like to keep it simple with some garlic, passata, prosciutto, red onion and Cheddar, and serve them with rocket. Roll 1 portion of dough into a pizza shape, place your fillings on one side, then fold the dough over and use a fork to seal the edges. Brush the whole calzone with garlic butter and either air fry for 12 minutes at 200°C or oven bake for 15 minutes at 200°C fan . When cooked, brush with garlic butter again.

Flatbreads

This is my favourite thing to do with this 2-ingredient dough. The frying process makes it super crispy on the outside but fluffy on the inside. Roll 1 portion of dough into a flatbread shape (like a long pizza) and fry with a little oil for 5 minutes on each side until golden brown.

Sesame bagels

These are perfect for a Saturday morning. When they're cooked, I like to crack an egg in the middle and cook for a further 3 minutes! Shape 1 dough portion into a circle and use your thumbs to make a hole in the middle. Sprinkle with sesame seeds, spray with oil and pop either into the air fryer for 12 minutes at 200°C or into a preheated oven for 15 minutes at 200°C fan.

Bread bowls for soup

These bowls are perfect for filling with a hearty soup. Shape 1 portion of dough into a circular loaf shape, spray with oil and either air fry at 200°C for 12 minutes or oven bake for 15 minutes at 200°C fan. When cooked and cooled, cut off the top of the bread to make a lid, scoop out the bread from inside and fill with soup. Put the lid back on. I like to roll the bread that was scooped out into little dough balls and put them in the soup.

Pizza bowls

Grease the outside of an ovenproof bowl with a little oil. Roll out 1 portion of the dough thinly and wrap it around the bowl to create a bowl shape. Tuck any loose edges into the inside of the bowl.

Cover the whole bowl with foil and pop it into the airfryer for 12 minutes at 200°C or into the oven for 20 minutes at 200°C fan. Remove and let it cool, then use a fork to remove the dough from the bowl. Fill the dough bowl with tomato pasta, shredded cheese and whatever toppings you like. I love prosciutto, rocket and Parmesan!

Garlic Parmesan skillet rolls

This is a fun thing to do with the dough, perfect for pasta night. You will need 3 portions of the dough, though, as it's a sharing dish. Roll the dough out and use a biscuit cutter (I use my daughters' playdoh one!) to make 3 small circle shapes from each portion (around 2½cm/1 inch thick). You should get 9 in total. Rub butter or oil all over a large ovenproof skillet, or a baking tray. Line the 9 dough circles out and use your thumb to create a dib in each circle. Bake in the oven for 10 minutes at 200°C fan. Make a garlic butter by combining 4 tablespoons of butter, 5 cloves of garlic, grated, a handful of chopped parsley, salt and pepper. Brush it all over the dough rolls, top with Parmesan, Cheddar and a sprinkle of parsley, and bake for another 5 minutes.

Air-Fryer

Feasts

Teriyaki Salmon Tacos

SERVES: 4 • TIME: 30 MINUTES

If you're not air frying salmon yet, you're missing out. It makes it super crispy and juicy. Add a teriyaki glaze to the mix and chop the salmon, and you get even more crispiness. I made these tacos for my family recently and they didn't even make it out of the kitchen.

1. Defrost your salmon fillets under cold running water. When fully defrosted, cut them into 2cm cubes. Place in a bowl with the rest of the salmon ingredients, except the teriyaki sauce and the oil.

2. Space the salmon cubes out in the air fryer and spray/drizzle with the oil.

3. Air fry at 180°C for 3 minutes, then open the air fryer drawer and brush the salmon with the teriyaki sauce. Air fry for another 2 minutes.

4. Make the lime sour cream by chopping the jalapeños, then mix them with the rest of the sour cream ingredients in a bowl and season them with salt.

5. Toast your tortillas using the open flame on your gas hob, or a hot frying pan, then layer with shredded cabbage, lime sour cream and the teriyaki salmon chunks.

6. Top with chilli flakes and sesame seeds and serve with pink pickled onions and sliced green chilli.

For the salmon

4 frozen salmon fillets
1 teaspoon onion powder
1 teaspoon garlic powder
½ teaspoon Cajun seasoning
salt and pepper
4 tablespoons teriyaki sauce
2 tablespoons olive oil

Lime sour cream

1 teaspoon pickled
  jalapeños
6 tablespoons sour cream
1 tablespoon jalapeño brine
juice and zest of 1 lime

For the tacos

8 small flour tortillas
a handful of shredded
  cabbage
chilli flakes
sesame seeds
pink pickled onions
1 mild green chilli

Cornflake Katsu Curry

SERVES: 4 • TIME: 35 MINUTES

Chicken katsu curry usually uses panko breadcrumbs, but cornflakes work just as well. The cornflakes are more golden and crunchy, which goes so nicely with the katsu curry sauce.

1. To make the sauce, chop the onion, garlic and carrots. Heat 1 tablespoon olive oil in a pan, add the onion and garlic and fry for 2 minutes, then add the carrots and fry slowly for 10 minutes, with a lid on if possible.

2. Stir in the flour and curry powder and cook for 1 minute, then slowly pour in the stock bit by bit. Add the honey and soy sauce, then reduce the heat and simmer for 20 minutes until thickened. Using a soup blender, blitz until smooth and keep warm.

3. Put the 100g of flour into a shallow bowl and season well. Crack the eggs into a second bowl, whisk and season well. Crush or blend the cornflakes and put them into a third bowl.

4. Place your chicken breasts on a piece of clingfilm and place more clingfilm over the top. Using a rolling pin or something similar, bash the chicken out to flatten it.

5. One by one, dip the chicken breasts first into the flour, then into the egg mixture, then into the cornflakes, shaking off any excess. Place them in the air fryer (you may have to do this in two batches), then drizzle or spray with oil and air fry at 170°C for 10–12 minutes, until crispy and cooked through.

6. Meanwhile, cook 50g of rice per person in salted boiling water for 15 minutes (or according to the packet instructions). Slice the spring onions.

7. Serve the rice with the chicken on top. Drizzle over the curry sauce. Scatter with the spring onions and sesame seeds.

100g flour
salt and pepper
2 eggs
200g cornflakes
4 chicken breasts
olive oil

For the sauce
1 onion
5 cloves of garlic
2 carrots
1 tablespoon olive oil
2 tablespoons plain flour
1 tablespoon curry powder
500ml chicken stock
2 teaspoons honey
1 tablespoon light soy sauce

To serve
200g jasmine rice
3 spring onions
sesame seeds
boiled edamame beans

Slow-Cooker
Feasts

Slow-Cooker Feasts

Slow cookers are the busy cook's best friend. Just add a handful of ingredients and let the magic of time and heat do their work, and you'll come back a few hours later to a house wafting with delicious flavours and aromas. Like air fryers, slow cookers are also a really economical way to cook when compared to the hob or oven, so you'll be saving on your energy bill as well as your food bill! Highlights from this chapter include juicy Beef Brisket Burrito Bowls (page 106) and Pulled Pork & Black Bean Chilli (page 110), as well as comforting classics like creamy Chicken Chasseur (page 114) and hearty Brisket Ragù (page 117).

Chicken Tortilla Soup

**SERVES: 4 • TIME: 20 MINUTES PREP,
6–8 HOURS SLOW COOKING**

*I've been so excited to show you this one. It's amazing. The perfect bowl
to warm up with on a winter's day. Made with loads of juicy vegetables
and shredded, slow-cooked chicken, it's hearty but healthy and so delicious.
Topped with plenty of sour cream and fresh coriander, and some crunchy
tortilla strips, this is a cosy meal that you can feel good about eating.*

1. Slice the red onion, and chop the garlic and chilli. Drain the tin of sweetcorn, but there is no need to drain the beans. Put the chicken thighs into the slow cooker with the rest of the soup ingredients. Add 1 teaspoon of salt and cook on low for 6–8 hours.

2. Slice the tortillas into long strips. Heat the olive oil in a frying pan and fry the strips until they are golden and crispy, then remove them and pat the oil off them with kitchen paper.

3. When the time is up, remove the chicken from the soup and shred it using two forks. Then put it back into the soup.

4. Pop your rice into the microwave to cook, then add it to the pot. Chop the coriander and add most of it to the pot with the tortilla strips.

5. Serve the soup in large bowls, with the tortilla strips stirred through, and top with sour cream, sliced avocado, chopped spring onion, the rest of the coriander and wedges of lime.

TIP:

Where possible, use your supermarket's budget essentials range. You'll be amazed by how much your shopping bill goes down and the quality of the produce is often very similar.

For the soup
1 red onion
3 cloves of garlic
1 small red chilli
1 tin of sweetcorn
1 x 400g tin of black beans
300g boneless, skinless chicken thighs
1 teaspoon ground cumin
1 teaspoon chilli powder
1 tablespoon chipotle paste/ seasoning or smoked paprika
1 x 400g tin of chopped tomatoes
500ml chicken stock
juice and zest of 1 lime

For the tortilla strips
4 regular corn or flour tortillas
6 tablespoons vegetable oil

To serve
100g pre-cooked micro-waveable long-grain rice
1 handful of fresh coriander
4 tablespoons sour cream
1 large avocado
1 spring onion
1 lime

Crispy Barbecue Chicken Tacos

**SERVES: 4 • TIME: 20 MINUTES PREP,
6–8 HOURS SLOW COOKING**

The kids will love these, and they're so easy to make. Shredded, juicy chicken in a smoky barbecue sauce, stuffed into crispy tortillas with loads of melted cheese oozing out. Apologies if the kids refuse to eat anything else after these!

1. Chop the garlic and slice the onion. Put the chicken thighs into the slow cooker with the garlic, onion, paprika, Cajun seasoning, chilli powder, barbecue sauce, passata, salt, pepper and 100ml of water, and cook on low for 8 hours (overnight is best).

2. When the time is up, use two forks to shred the chicken in the slow cooker.

3. Preheat the oven to 200°C fan and oil a baking tray. Put 8 small tortillas on the tray (you may need 2 trays).

4. Place a handful of cheese on each tortilla, then spoon over some of the chicken mix from the slow cooker and place the tray(s) in the oven for 10 minutes.

5. When cooked and super crispy, remove the trays, fold the tacos over and serve with soured cream, lime wedges, red onion and hot sauce, if you like it.

4 cloves of garlic

1 large white onion

6 boneless, skinless chicken thighs

1 tablespoon smoked paprika

1 tablespoon Cajun seasoning

1 teaspoon chilli powder

4 tablespoons barbecue sauce

4–6 tablespoons passata

salt and pepper

8 small flour tortillas

320g grated Cheddar cheese

150ml soured cream

lime wedges

1 small red onion, chopped

2–6 tablespoons of hot sauce (optional)

Creamy Chicken Soup + Roasted Mushrooms

**SERVES: 4–6 • TIME: 20 MINUTES PREP,
8 HOURS SLOW COOKING**

This is the cosiest, heartiest bowl of chicken soup you'll ever find, and it's mostly made from essentials that you'll have in the cupboard. It's the easiest dinner to prepare! Just throw everything into the slow cooker and you're done. The roasted mushrooms take only minutes to make but add just the right amount of texture. It's creamy, warming, and every spoonful is so delicious.

1. Chop the onion, carrots and 4 cloves of garlic. Set the carrots aside, then put the onion and garlic into a slow cooker with the chicken, Dijon mustard, Worcestershire sauce and the chicken stock. Season with salt and pepper and cook for 8 hours on low.

2. Towards the end of the 8 hours, add the carrots to the slow cooker. Preheat your oven to 200°C fan. Quarter the mushrooms and grate the remaining 2 garlic cloves. Mix them together and spread them on a baking tray with a drizzle of oil and half of the thyme leaves and roast for 30 minutes. When ready, remove from the oven and set aside.

3. When the 8 hours is up and the carrots are cooked, use two forks to shred the chicken in the slow cooker. Stir in the cream and the cheese, and add half the roasted mushrooms. Pop the rice into the microwave to heat through, then stir into the soup.

4. Spoon the soup into large bowls and top with the rest of the roasted mushrooms and fresh thyme. Serve with crusty bread.

1 large white onion

6 carrots

6 cloves of garlic

6 boneless, skinless chicken thighs

1 teaspoon Dijon mustard

2 tablespoons Worcestershire sauce

1.5 litres chicken stock

salt and pepper

250g chestnut mushrooms

olive oil

1 teaspoon fresh thyme leaves

250ml single cream

150g grated Cheddar cheese

150g cooked rice (1 packet of microwaveable rice is best)

Lasagne Soup

**SERVES: 4 • TIME: 15 MINUTES PREP,
6 HOURS SLOW COOKING, 15 MINUTES TO SERVE**

Creamy, slow-cooked lasagne soup. Great for when you're wanting lasagne, but not all the work that goes into it. Beef simmered with vegetables, Italian spices, a creamy tomato sauce and lasagne ribbons. Finish each bowl with a sprinkle of Parmesan and serve with garlic bread.

1. Chop the onion, peppers and garlic and put them into the slow cooker.

2. Add the mince and season with salt and pepper. Add the tomato purée, basil, oregano, thyme, and the chilli flakes if using. Add the chopped tomatoes and the stock, and give everything a good stir. Cook for 6 hours on low.

3. Towards the end, put 8 lasagne sheets into a pan of boiling water and simmer for 5 minutes. Remove them from the water and cut them up lengthways into long pieces. You should get 4 slices from every sheet. Put the slices into the soup to finish cooking – they will need another 10–15 minutes on a low heat, until al dente. Before serving, stir in the cream and a big handful of Parmesan and cook for another 10 minutes to warm through. Season to taste.

4. Serve in large bowls with garlic bread, and sprinkle Parmesan on top, with more chilli flakes if you like.

1 onion

2 red peppers

6 cloves of garlic or 2 tablespoons garlic purée

250g beef or chicken mince

salt and pepper

1 tablespoon tomato purée

1 tablespoon dried basil

1 tablespoon dried oregano

1 tablespoon dried thyme

½ teaspoon chilli flakes (optional)

1 x 400g tin of chopped tomatoes

800ml chicken stock

8 lasagne sheets

100ml single cream

a handful of Parmesan cheese, and extra for topping

Chicken Chasseur

**SERVES: 4 • TIME: 10 MINUTES PREP,
8 HOURS SLOW COOKING, 10 MINUTES TO SERVE**

*A hearty, French-inspired, rustic dish never goes out of style. My mum used
to cook it for me, her mum used to cook it for her, and I cook it for my girls.
It's a dish that makes me sleep happy, as the girls demolish it every time, it's
packed full of goodness and it's slow cooked, which means I haven't spent
hours in the kitchen preparing and cooking it. I serve it with a warm buttered
baguette.*

1. Chop the mushrooms, onion and garlic. Cut the chicken thighs into large chunks. Pick and chop the thyme leaves. Chop the bacon rashers and fry them in the butter in a frying pan until crispy.

2. Put the bacon into your slow cooker with all the other ingredients and give everything a good stir. Cook on low for 8 hours. If the sauce looks thin, transfer it to a pan, bring to a boil and cook for 10 minutes to reduce.

3. Serve with rice, mashed potatoes or warm crusty bread.

250g mushrooms

1 large white onion

3 cloves of garlic

8 boneless, skinless chicken thighs

a handful of fresh thyme

4 smoked bacon rashers

1 tablespoon butter

1 x 400g tin of chopped tomatoes

2 tablespoons plain flour

2 tablespoons Worcestershire sauce

1 tablespoon tomato purée

1 tablespoon smoked paprika

1 bay leaf

300ml chicken stock

150ml dry white wine (optional)

Brisket Ragù

**SERVES: 4 • TIME: 10 MINUTES PREP,
8 HOURS SLOW COOKING, 10 MINUTES TO SERVE**

I've turned this classic cosy recipe into something a bit more special. Brisket cooked gently in the slow cooker makes the most tender and delicious shredded beef ever. This recipe creates a rich tomato sauce for the beef and pasta to mix into.

1. Put your brisket into a frying pan with a little oil and fry on all sides to seal the meat.

2. Chop the onion, carrot, celery and garlic. Put your brisket into the slow cooker with all the ingredients except the pasta and the Parmesan and cook on low for 8 hours.

3. When cooked, remove the brisket from the slow cooker and shred it with two forks. If the sauce looks thin then transfer it to a pan and bring to the boil to reduce for 10 minutes. Put the shredded beef back into the sauce.

4. Cook your pasta according to the packet instructions, then drain it and add it to the pot of meat and sauce.

5. Serve with grated Parmesan.

1 x 1kg joint of brisket
olive oil
1 onion
1 carrot
1 celery stick
5 cloves of garlic
2 x 400g tins of plum tomatoes
200ml red wine
250ml chicken stock
1 teaspoon dried oregano
1 bay leaf
320g pappardelle pasta
50g grated Parmesan cheese
salt and pepper

TIP:

Embrace click and collect! I always use it for my weekly shop. At most supermarkets you don't pay any extra (as you do for home delivery) and it helps you avoid impulse purchases.

Carnitas Tacos

SERVES: 4 (2 CARNITAS TACOS EACH)
• TIME: 5 MINUTES PREP, 8 HOURS SLOW COOKING

In my eyes, every tortilla dreams of being stuffed with carnitas. Carnitas are just Mexican seasoned slow-cooked pork, gently shredded, then pan-fried to golden, crispy perfection. Carnitas have that perfect combination of juicy and crispy that is irresistible, and the best part is that they only take 5 minutes to prepare. The slow cooker does all the hard work!

1. Place your pork shoulder in a bowl, drizzle with oil and add the chilli flakes, Cajun seasoning, cumin, chilli powder, oregano and cinnamon with plenty of salt and pepper. Using your hands, coat the meat with the spices.

2. Slice up your onion and garlic and put them in the slow cooker, then put the pork on top, add the pineapple and lime juices and cook on low for 8 hours.

3. When the meat is cooked, remove it from the slow cooker, place in a bowl and shred it with two forks. Transfer the meat to a frying pan, spoon over some of the juices and the barbecue sauce, then fry for 5 minutes, until golden, to crisp it up.

4. Make a lime sour cream by mixing the sour cream, lime juice and a little lime zest in a bowl and grating in 1 clove of garlic. Chop the coriander.

5. Heat your flour tortillas on the naked flame of the hob. Add some meat and lime sour cream, top with the chopped coriander, then fold over and serve with the lime wedges.

700g pork shoulder
olive oil
1 teaspoon chilli flakes
1 tablespoon Cajun seasoning
1 teaspoon ground cumin
1 teaspoon chilli powder
1 teaspoon dried oregano
½ teaspoon ground cinnamon
salt and pepper
1 large white onion
4 cloves of garlic
250ml pineapple juice
juice of 1 lime
2 tablespoons BBQ sauce

For the lime sour cream
100ml sour cream
½ a lime, juice and zest
1 clove of garlic, grated

To serve
a handful of fresh coriander
8 small flour tortillas
lime wedges

Greek Chicken Gyros Traybake

SERVES: 4 • TIME: 45 MINUTES

I think about proper saucy, crispy gyros a lot. They are the ultimate comfort food in my eyes. I spent a season in Zante when I was younger and used to get them every night on the way home. All the flavours and textures are so tasty together, so I thought why not cook them together!

1. Dice the chicken breasts and put them into a bowl. Grate 6 cloves of garlic and add to the bowl with 75ml of yoghurt, the juice of 1 lemon, 1 tablespoon of smoked paprika, 1 tablespoon of oregano, a generous drizzle of oil and plenty of salt and pepper.

2. Slice the red onions and add them to the bowl, then cover the bowl and leave the chicken to marinate in the fridge for as long as possible – overnight is best, but 15 minutes will be fine.

3. Preheat your oven to 180°C fan. Slice your potatoes (skin on) into long chips and lay them out on a baking tray. Sprinkle them with a tablespoon each of smoked paprika and oregano, drizzle with oil and add plenty of salt and pepper.

4. Spread the marinated chicken mixture on a second baking tray, and pop both trays into the oven for 20 minutes. Take the trays out, give them a good shake, then put them back in for 10 minutes.

5. Meanwhile, make the tzatziki. Shred the cucumber and grate the remaining 2 cloves of garlic. Pop the feta cheese, the remaining 75ml of yoghurt, the grated garlic, a little salt and the juice of the second lemon into a blender and blend until creamy. Stir through half the grated cucumber.

6. Shred the lettuce and slice the tomato.

7. Remove the chips and chicken from the oven. Warm your pitta breads in a toaster, then add a spoonful of tzatziki to each pitta. Layer a few chips on, then some chicken. Add some lettuce, tomato and the rest of the cucumber, and add hot sauce if you like it.

3 chicken breasts
8 cloves of garlic
150ml full fat Greek yoghurt
juice of 2 lemons
2 tablespoons smoked paprika
2 tablespoons dried oregano
olive oil
salt and pepper
2 red onions
2 large white potatoes
1 cucumber
½ a block of feta cheese
1 handful of baby gem lettuce leaves
1 beef tomato
8 pitta breads
hot sauce (optional)

Cajun Cream Prawn Pasta

SERVES: 4 • TIME: 30 MINUTES

I used to eat this all the time when I worked at that well-known American restaurant through uni. It used to be my incentive to actually go to work after being out or doing uni work all night. It's so hearty and tasty, and the prawns go perfectly with the creamy Cajun sauce. I've re-created it perfectly here, and I don't know if I love it or hate it, as when I eat it I'm back in those days, having it all the time!

1. Put the prawns into a bowl and mix with the lemon juice, smoked paprika and 1 tablespoon of Cajun seasoning. Let the prawns marinate for at least 15 minutes (but overnight in the fridge is best).

2. Cook the pasta in salted boiling water according to the instructions on the packet, then drain and set aside.

3. Meanwhile, finely chop the garlic and cut the red pepper and onion into small chunks. Return the pan that you cooked the pasta in to the heat then fry the garlic, pepper and onion in a little oil for 5 minutes. Add the cayenne pepper and the prawns with their marinade, and cook for another 5 minutes.

4. Stir the cream and chicken stock into the prawns, then return the cooked pasta to the pan and stir through the grated cheese until everything is well combined.

5. Spoon into bowls and serve with fresh basil leaves scattered over.

200g raw prawns
juice of 1 lemon
1 tablespoon smoked paprika
1½ tablespoons Cajun seasoning
320g penne pasta
4 cloves of garlic
1 red pepper
1 white onion
olive oil
½ teaspoon cayenne pepper
250ml single cream
150ml chicken stock
150g grated Cheddar cheese
a handful of fresh basil

TIP:

Buy potted herbs and you can use them again and again, as long as you look after them! If you do have leftover cut herbs, chop them into ice cube trays, cover with a little water and freeze. You can then throw the frozen cubes straight into dishes as needed.

Stovetop Tomato Soup + Toasted Cheese Pockets

MAKES: 4 BOWLS • TIME: 40 MINUTES

Recipes like this sometimes come to me when I'm really fancying something easy to make. So simple but so hearty, nourishing and full of flavour. The melty cheese toasties make this dish. Surprise the kids with it and they'll be so happy!

1. Preheat the oven to 200°C fan.

2. Chop the tomatoes, onion, garlic and red pepper and lay them on a baking tray. Sprinkle the dried oregano over the top, then drizzle with oil and bake for 20 minutes, giving the tray a good shake halfway through.

3. Chop the basil and parsley. Put the stock in the jug of a blender, then add the roasted veg from the tray and 1 tablespoon each of the chopped basil and parsley. Add the cream, butter and sugar, then, blend everything together until smooth.

4. To create your toasted cheese pockets, layer the cheese between 2 slices of bread. Then, using a box grater or even a pint glass or something else of a similar width, push down on the sandwich like a blunt cookie cutter – the force should seal the edges. Remove the crusts from around the edge, then pop this pocket into a sandwich toaster for a few minutes to melt the cheese.

5. Serve the soup in bowls, with a little chopped basil sprinkled on top, and with the toasted cheese pockets alongside.

1kg tomatoes (400g cherry tomatoes, 300g large tomatoes, 300g vine-ripened tomatoes)

1 white onion

4 cloves of garlic

1 red pepper

½ teaspoon dried oregano

olive oil

a handful of fresh basil

a handful of fresh parsley

200ml chicken (or veg) stock

100ml single cream

50g butter

1 teaspoon sugar

For the toasted cheese pockets

200g grated Cheddar

2 large slices of white sandwich bread per person

Smoky Italian Beef & Ricotta Meatballs

MAKES: 4 BOWLS • TIME: 40 MINUTES

These ricotta meatballs swimming in a smoky arrabbiata sauce are everything! This is the only Italian meatball recipe you'll ever need. Top them with loads of melty cheese and serve with warm bread to mop up that sauce. Properly delicious.

1. To make the sauce, chop the red onion and grate the garlic. Heat 1 tablespoon of olive oil in a frying pan and add the chilli flakes, onion and garlic. After about a minute, add half the basil leaves and gently wilt them in the oil, then add the chopped tomatoes and smoked paprika and leave to simmer for 5–10 minutes. Season with salt and pepper.

2. To make the meatballs, chop the parsley and put it into a bowl with the beef mince, the rest of the meatball ingredients and plenty of salt and pepper. Mix together with your hands, then shape the mixture into 16 small meatballs. Add them to the pan of arrabbiata sauce, then place a lid on top and cook for 15 minutes.

3. When the meatballs are cooked, slice the mozzarella and ricotta and lay the slices on top of the meatballs in the pan, then cover with the lid and let the steam melt the cheese. Top with the remaining fresh basil.

4. Serve with warm bread and garlic butter, or spaghetti.

For the smoky arrabbiata sauce
1 red onion
2 cloves of garlic
olive oil
½ teaspoon chilli flakes
2 handfuls of fresh basil
2 x 400g tins of chopped tomatoes
1 teaspoon smoked paprika
salt and pepper

For the meatballs
a small handful of fresh parsley
500g beef mince
2 tablespoons fresh or shop-bought breadcrumbs
150g ricotta
1 tablespoon dried oregano
1 tablespoon smoked paprika
1 large egg
½ teaspoon baking soda

125g fresh mozzarella
150g ricotta

Indian Traybake

SERVES: 4 • TIME: 50 MINUTES

This Indian traybake was one of the first things I made on my Instagram page, and one of the first things people started remaking. Indian flavours are so delicious, but a curry is not always what you fancy. The Indian spices with the chicken and vegetables in this traybake are so tasty and fragrant, and not too spicy either, so the kids will really love this one. I serve it with warm naans and with mint yoghurt drizzled all over everything.

1. Preheat the oven to 190°C fan.

2. Chop the chicken and all the vegetables – you want everything to be chunky. Leave the tomatoes whole.

3. Drain the chickpeas, then put them into a large roasting dish with the chopped vegetables. Try not to overcrowd it, as the ingredients will go soggy – use two roasting dishes if you have to, as you want everything to be touching the dish so it crisps up.

4. Crush the garlic and add to the dish, then sprinkle the spices over everything.

5. Drizzle some oil over the top and add plenty of salt and pepper.

6. Pop into the oven for 30–40 minutes, until all the veg is cooked through and roasted nicely. Halfway through, take the dish out of the oven and give it a good shake.

7. While the traybake is cooking, finely chop the mint and mix it with the yoghurt and lemon juice in a bowl to make a mint dressing.

8. Serve the chicken and vegetables with the yoghurt dressing drizzled over the top.

500g boneless, skinless chicken thighs or skinless breasts

500g baby potatoes

250g mushrooms

1 red pepper

1 red onion

250g cherry tomatoes

½ a 400g tin of chickpeas

6 cloves of garlic

2 tablespoons curry powder

1 teaspoon chilli powder

1 tablespoon smoked paprika

oil

salt and pepper

For the yoghurt dressing

a handful of fresh mint

8 tablespoons Greek yoghurt

2 tablespoons lemon juice

Red Thai Salmon Traybake

SERVES: 4 • TIME: 30 MINUTES

This flavour-packed dish is probably the quickest yet tastiest meal in the whole book. The red Thai curry paste mixed with the creamy coconut milk and zesty lime juice soak into everything while the salmon is in the oven. I like to place the whole dish on the table for everyone to tuck into with forks.

1. Preheat the oven to 200°C fan.

2. Put the rice into an ovenproof dish and place the salmon fillets on top.

3. Chop the pak choi and place on top of the rice.

4. Chop the red pepper and place on top of the pak choi.

5. In a jug, mix the red Thai curry paste with the coconut milk and the juice of 1 lime. Adjust the amount of curry paste to taste. Pour the mixture over the salmon and place in the oven for 20 minutes, or until the salmon is cooked through.

6. Serve in bowls, topped with chopped spring onions and wedges of lime, slices of red chilli and sprinkled with sesame seeds.

2 packets of precooked microwaveable rice

4 salmon fillets, skin on (pre-marinated salmon is best)

1 pak choi

1 red pepper

3 tablespoons red Thai curry paste

1 x 400ml tin of coconut milk

juice of 1 lime

To serve

2 spring onions

2 limes

sliced red chilli

sesame seeds (we used a mix of black and white sesame seeds)

Southwest Dirty Rice

SERVES: 4 • TIME: 45 MINUTES

This dish is so easy and smells amazing while it's cooking. The rice slowly simmers with the southwest spices, chorizo and vegetables until all the juices are soaked up. It's unbelievably tasty. I make sure I cook extra so there's enough for the next day.

1. Chop the red peppers, onion, chilli, garlic and cherry tomatoes. In a pan, fry your beef mince and chorizo in a little oil with the garlic, cumin, 1 tablespoon of smoked paprika and a pinch of salt and pepper.

2. Once cooked through, add the turmeric, oregano, three-quarters of the cherry tomatoes, the red peppers, onion and chilli and cook for 5 minutes, until the veg are soft.

3. Add the tomato purée, the juice of 1 lime and three-quarters of the vegetable stock. Then add your rice and ½ teaspoon of salt.

4. Place a lid on the pot and simmer on a low heat for 15 minutes, adding more stock throughout if it needs it. Check the rice, and if not soft, add a little more stock and cook for 5 minutes more, or until the rice is cooked and the stock has been absorbed.

5. Make a southwest sour cream by mixing the sour cream with half a teaspoon of smoked paprika, a squeeze of half a lime and salt to taste.

6. Once the rice is cooked and all the liquid has been absorbed, serve in a large dish, topped with the rest of the cherry tomatoes and some chopped red onion, with the southwest sour cream on the side and the remaining lime half to squeeze over.

2 red peppers
1 onion
1 fresh red chilli
4 cloves of garlic
200g cherry tomatoes
250g beef mince
200g chorizo ring, cut into small chunks
olive oil
1 teaspoon ground cumin
1 tablespoon smoked paprika, plus ½ teaspoon
salt and pepper
1 teaspoon ground turmeric
1 teaspoon dried oregano
1 tablespoon tomato purée
2 limes
500ml vegetable stock
250g long-grain rice
300g fresh sour cream
chopped red onion, to serve

Middle Eastern Style Chicken + Whipped Feta

SERVES: 4 • TIME: 40 MINUTES

Middle Eastern spices are great for a midweek family meal, as they're fragrant and flavourful but not too hot. The creamy whipped feta really completes this meal.

1. Preheat the oven to 180°C fan. Chop the garlic and parsley and place in a bowl with the rest of the marinade ingredients.

2. Put the chicken drumsticks on a large baking tray. Cut each onion into 6 wedges, halve the potatoes, then add them all to the tray and drizzle the marinade over everything. Use your hands to mix it all up, then slice the lemon and lay it over the top. Drizzle with olive oil.

3. Bake in the oven for 45 minutes, stirring once or twice, then switch to the grill setting for 5 minutes to crisp everything up.

4. To make the whipped feta, put the feta and its brine into a small food processor or blender, add the yoghurt and lemon juice, and blitz until smooth. Add a splash of water if needed.

5. Spoon the whipped feta on to a serving plate and spread it out into a crescent shape, using the back of a spoon.

6. Layer the chicken and potatoes on top of the whipped feta and top with a scattering of mint and parsley leaves.

8 chicken drumsticks
3 small white onions
400g baby potatoes
1 lemon
2 tablespoons olive oil

For the marinade
6 cloves of garlic
1 tablespoon fresh parsley
4 tablespoons Greek yoghurt
2 teaspoons smoked paprika
2 teaspoons ground cumin
1 teaspoon salt
½ teaspoon onion powder
1 teaspoon ginger purée
juice of 1 lemon
4 tablespoons olive oil

For the whipped feta
200g feta cheese (including brine)
6 tablespoons Greek yoghurt
juice of 1 lemon

To serve
Handful of picked mint and parsley leaves

Chicken noodle soup

Chop ½ a carrot, ½ a white onion and 1 celery stick, then put into a pan with butter and fry for 5–6 minutes, until soft. Add 2 chopped cloves of garlic, 1 bay leaf and a few sprigs of thyme, then pour in 300ml of chicken stock. Add a handful of fusilli pasta and cook for 15 minutes. Stir in 1 portion of shredded chicken, and serve with warm buttered bread.

Lime chicken tacos

To make 3 tacos, put 1 portion of shredded chicken into a frying pan with 1 teaspoon of butter, ½ a chopped onion and ½ a chopped green pepper. Cook until the chicken has blackened and the veg are soft, then stir in a little lime zest, the juice of 1 whole lime, 1 teaspoon of honey and some chilli flakes. Make some quick lime slaw (see page 181), then spoon the chicken mixture on to small flour tortillas and add the slaw and some chopped coriander.

Cajun quesadillas

Fry ½ a chopped red onion and ½ a chopped red pepper with 2 chopped cloves of garlic, ½ teaspoon of smoked paprika and ½ teaspoon of Cajun seasoning, until soft. Add 1 portion of shredded chicken with some hot sauce and a teaspoon of butter, and fry for 5 minutes. Heat a little oil in a separate pan and add 1 large flour tortilla. Spoon 2 tablespoons of the chicken mixture on to the tortilla, along with a handful of grated Cheddar. Fold the tortilla over and press down to make a quesadilla. Fry for 5 minutes on a low heat, then flip over and fry the other side for 5 minutes. Serve with sour cream and rice.

Busy-day chipotle fajitas or nachos

To make 2 fajitas, fry a handful of chopped mushrooms and ½ a chopped red onion with a little oil until soft. Add 1 portion of shredded chicken with a teaspoon of butter and fry until blackened. Add ½ teaspoon of chipotle paste or 1 teaspoon of chipotle seasoning and 2 tablespoons of barbecue sauce, and combine. Serve in a bowl, with flour tortillas, cheese, soured cream, guacamole and salsa on the side.

Comfort-Food

Feasts

Comfort-Food Feasts

If I had to pick a favourite chapter to cook from, this would be it. This is the kind of hug-in-a-bowl food that calls out to me on a daily basis and can immediately perk me up if I'm feeling low. In this chapter you'll find a mix of comfort classics, as well as thrifty fakeaways that will stop you reaching for the takeaway menu on a Friday night. Highlights include mouth-watering Sloppy Joe Tacos with Dirty Rice (page 178) and Double Candied Bacon & Brie Burgers (page 186) as well as creamy Speedy Coconut Butter Chicken (page 182) and deliciously oozy Smoky Enchilada Bake (page 201).

Moroccan Chicken Feta-Filled Flatbreads

MAKES: 4 FLATBREADS • TIME: 50 MINUTES

This 2-ingredient dough is so versatile, but making it into flatbreads is the best. They cook super quickly, crispy and golden on the outside but doughy and fluffy on the inside. Add some melted feta and you've got a real showstopper. I love them this way, topped with chicken, and with plenty of sauce to mop up.

1. To make the feta-filled flatbreads, combine the yoghurt and flour in a mixing bowl with a pinch of salt, and mix together with your hands until you have a consistency that doesn't stick to your hands. Divide the dough into 4 balls.

2. Lightly flour the work surface and roll each ball out into a circle, no bigger than your hand, and place 50g of crumbled feta cheese in the middle of each one. Pull the sides into the middle one by one so that all the cheese is covered, pinching the dough together to make sure the cheese is fully enclosed. Flip the dough over and roll it out into a flatbread shape.

3. To make the Moroccan chicken, preheat the oven to 190°C fan. Chop the red onion and red pepper, finely chop the garlic and halve the mushrooms. Drain the chickpeas. Slice the chicken breasts and put them into a roasting dish with the garlic, red onion, red pepper and mushrooms. Scatter the cherry tomatoes on top.

4. Sprinkle the thyme, harissa paste and smoked paprika over everything and drizzle with oil. Season with salt and pepper and bake in the oven for 25 minutes, giving the dish a good shake halfway through. Add the chickpeas and stir through, then cook for a final 5 minutes.

5. While the chicken is cooking, pan fry the flatbreads one at a time: in a little oil for 5 minutes, turning them halfway.

→

For the flatbreads
300ml Greek yoghurt
450g self-raising flour
salt
200g feta cheese
olive oil

For the Moroccan chicken topping
1 red onion
1 red pepper
3 cloves of garlic
200g mushrooms
½ x 400g tin of chickpeas
4 chicken breasts
250g cherry tomatoes
1 tablespoon dried thyme
1 teaspoon harissa paste
1 tablespoon smoked paprika
olive oil
salt and pepper
1 teaspoon chilli flakes

For the mint yoghurt
250ml Greek yoghurt
1 tablespoon lemon juice
1 teaspoon mint sauce
1 clove of garlic

6. To make the mint yoghurt, put the yoghurt, lemon juice and mint sauce into a bowl and grate in the garlic. Mix together and set aside.

7. Remove the dish of chicken and veg from the oven and give it a good stir. Layer the chicken on to your warm flatbreads, drizzle with the mint dressing, and finish with a sprinkling of chilli flakes.

SPRUCE IT UP!

I often make a big batch of this dough and freeze portions for later (see page 54). A tub of natural yoghurt and a pack of flour will cost around £1, and you'll end up with at least 10 portions!

Peanut Satay Chicken Noodles

SERVES: 4 • TIME: 30 MINUTES

This stir-fried coconutty peanut sauce tastes just like the satay chicken you get at the Chinese. Such a simple sauce, but mixed with noodles, chicken and veg it makes a bowl of slurp-worthy deliciousness.

1. Chop the garlic, ginger, spring onions and red pepper. Season the chicken with salt and pepper, then cut it into cubes and fry in a little oil with the garlic and ginger until golden.

2. Meanwhile mix all the satay sauce ingredients in a bowl.

3. Once your chicken is cooked through, add the mushrooms and cook for a few minutes, then add the spring onions and red pepper. You want these to stay crunchy, so only cook them for 2 minutes.

4. Meanwhile, cook your noodles in salted boiling water according to the packet instructions, and drain.

5. Add the satay sauce to the chicken and veg, then add your drained noodles.

6. Chop the spring onion, coriander and the chilli (if using) and sprinkle over the noodles to serve.

6 cloves of garlic
1 knob of fresh ginger
3 spring onions
1 red pepper
300g chicken breast mini fillets
salt and pepper
oil
250g button mushrooms
1 packet of medium dried egg noodles (any noodles will work)

For the satay sauce
1 tablespoon curry powder
3 tablespoons soy sauce
3 tablespoons peanut butter
3 tablespoons honey
juice of 1 lime
½ x 400ml tin of coconut milk

To serve
1 spring onion
a handful of fresh coriander
1 fresh chilli (optional)

Mexican Halloumi Taco Bowls

SERVES: 4 • TIME: 45 MINUTES

I feel like these halloumi taco bowls are my trademark dish. They're one of the first budget recipes I made that people fell in love with, and they're still re-created to this day. Super easy to make, but they look impressive and taste delish!

1. To make the tortilla bowls, rub oil all over the outside of a small round oven-safe bowl. Make sure it's really oily all over.

2. Place your bowl upside down, then place a whole flour tortilla wrap over it. Press the tortilla tightly around the shape of the bowl, then wrap the whole thing in foil. Repeat with the rest of the tortillas, then place either in an air fryer on 200°C for 10 minutes, or in a preheated oven at 180°C fan for 10 minutes, or until golden. Remove the foil and bowl and set the tortilla bowls on a rack to cool down.

3. Meanwhile, slice the peppers and red onion and drain the chickpeas. Put them all on a baking tray. Coat them with half the smoked paprika and Cajun seasoning, season with salt and pepper and drizzle with oil. Bake at 200°C for 20 minutes.

4. Slice the halloumi and sprinkle the other half of the smoked paprika over the slices, then fry in a pan with a little oil until golden on both sides.

5. Place the rice, baked vegetables, chickpeas and tomatoes in separate quarters of the tortilla bowls. Add fresh avocado or guacamole and tuck the fried halloumi in the top.

6. Put the yoghurt into a separate bowl with the smoked paprika and Cajun seasoning and mix together to make a dressing. Drizzle the dressing over the tacos and finish with chopped coriander and some hot sauce if you like it spicy!

olive oil

4 large tortilla wraps

2 peppers

1 red onion

½ x 400g tin of chickpeas

1 tablespoon smoked paprika

1 tablespoon Cajun seasoning

salt and pepper

225g halloumi

1 pack of pre-cooked Mexican rice

100g cherry tomatoes

1 x 150g tub of guacamole or 1 avocado

To serve

4 tablespoons natural yoghurt

1 teaspoon smoked paprika

1 teaspoon Cajun seasoning

chopped fresh coriander

hot sauce (optional)

Creamy Coconut & Peanut Laksa

SERVES: 4 • TIME: 20 MINUTES

Soup doesn't have to be boring. This creamy coconut and peanut laksa is my favourite thing to eat at the moment. It's so simple and easy to make, but flavourful and aromatic. You'll make this over and over again.

1. If using the oven, preheat it to 200°C fan.

2. Season the salmon fillets with the chilli flakes, smoked paprika, garlic powder and a pinch of salt, then drizzle with olive oil. Roast in the oven for 15 minutes, until crispy, or air fry on 180°C for 8 minutes.

3. While the salmon is cooking, chop 2 of the spring onions. Heat the vegetable oil and curry paste in a saucepan for 2 minutes. Add the spring onions and mix, then tip in the coconut milk and stir in the peanut butter.

4. Pour in the stock, then add the noodles and mangetout and simmer for 5 minutes, until the noodles have softened. Add the beansprouts, juice of a lime, the honey, soy sauce and fish sauce and mix well.

5. Chop the coriander and the remaining spring onion.

6. Divide the noodles between four bowls and add plenty of sauce. Put the salmon on top, and add the chopped coriander, beansprouts, spring onion, lime wedges, more chilli flakes and the sesame seeds.

TIP:

Look out for meal kits that contain some of these spices ready measured out. They will work out a lot cheaper than buying the ingredients individually and often contain just the right amount.

4 skinless salmon fillets

1 teaspoon chilli flakes, plus extra to garnish

1 tablespoon smoked paprika

1 tablespoon garlic powder

salt

olive oil

3 spring onions

1 tablespoon vegetable oil

3 tablespoons Thai red curry paste, or to taste

1 x 400ml tin of coconut milk

1 heaped tablespoon smooth peanut butter

350ml chicken stock

200g dried egg noodles

150g mangetout

large handful of beansprouts

2 limes

1 tablespoon honey

1 tablespoon dark soy sauce

2 tablespoons fish sauce

a handful of fresh coriander

1 tablespoon sesame seeds

Smoked Pancetta & Baked Feta Spaghetti

SERVES: 4 • TIME: 30 MINUTES

One of the simplest yet tastiest recipes in the book. A whole slab of feta baked with sweet cherry tomatoes and loads of garlic gives you a heavenly sauce, and the smoked pancetta just makes it.

1. Preheat the oven to 200°C fan.

2. Chop the onion and pancetta, put them into a frying pan and cook for 10 minutes, until the onions are caramelized from the fat of the pancetta.

3. Meanwhile, grate the garlic and chop 8 of the basil leaves. Put the feta in the centre of an ovenproof dish and arrange the tomatoes all around it. Drizzle with olive oil, top with the chopped garlic and basil, season with salt and pepper and cook in the middle of the oven for 30 minutes.

4. Meanwhile, cook the pasta. When you drain it, reserve a glass of the starchy water – this is important for the sauce.

5. When everything is cooked, add the baked feta and tomatoes to the pancetta and onions. Chop another 4 basil leaves and add to the pan, then add the pasta, stirring in the starchy pasta water to give you a creamy, silky sauce. Season with salt and pepper.

6. Top with Parmesan, a squeeze of lemon and a sprinkling of chilli flakes.

1 large onion

150g smoked pancetta

5 cloves of garlic

1 handful of basil

200g feta cheese

360g cherry tomatoes

olive oil

salt and pepper

320g spaghetti

1 handful of Parmesan cheese

1 lemon

1 teaspoon of chilli flakes

Teriyaki Pad Thai

SERVES: 4 • TIME: 30 MINUTES

Noodles are my weakness. They're my go-to meal, and something I fancy no matter what. They're so versatile, but stir-fried with loads of chicken and veg and a sticky teriyaki sauce is when they perform best, in my opinion.

1. In a frying pan or wok, heat the vegetable oil and fry your chicken mince with the garlic, ginger and Chinese 5-spice for 5–10 minutes, until cooked through.

2. If you are using dried noodles, cook them according to the packet instructions.

3. Finely slice the red pepper and chop the pak choi and spring onions. Add these to the pan of chicken mince with the soy sauce, fish sauce and teriyaki sauce and cook for a couple of minutes.

4. Chop the peanuts and finely chop the coriander and the other spring onion.

5. Beat the eggs in a bowl. Move the meat and veg to one side of the pan and add the eggs. Let them cook for 1 minute, then scramble the egg and mix it with the meat and veg.

6. Add the noodles and mix everything together well.

7. Finish with a scattering of peanuts, chilli flakes and spring onions.

1 tablespoon vegetable oil

250g chicken mince

1 tablespoon garlic purée

1 tablespoon ginger purée

½ teaspoon Chinese 5-spice

200g rice noodles (wide, flat ones are best)

1 red pepper

1 pak choi

2 spring onions

4 tablespoons light soy sauce

1 tablespoon fish sauce

2 tablespoons teriyaki sauce

2 eggs

To finish

a handful of roasted peanuts

1 spring onion

1 teaspoon chilli flakes

Crispy Sesame Beef Fried Rice

SERVES: 4 • TIME: 15 MINUTES

Two of my favourite takeaway dishes combined – crispy chilli beef and fried rice made into a delicious, high-protein and healthier option. It takes only 15 minutes to knock up this dish, which is a good thing, as I'm sure you'll want to make it a weekly staple!

1. Boil 4 of the eggs for 6 minutes, then place them in iced water to stop the cooking process.

2. Beat the remaining egg. Heat 1 tablespoon of oil in a frying pan and add the egg. Stir to scramble then remove to a plate.

3. Chop the garlic. Put 2 tablespoons of oil into a frying pan, add the beef mince and ginger purée and fry for around 10 minutes, until super crispy.

4. Finely chop the spring onions and add three-quarters of them to the beef with the soy sauce and teriyaki sauce.

5. Add the rice to your crispy beef, then chop the pak choi and add it to the pan. Fry for 5 minutes and add the scrambled egg back into the pan.

6. Serve in bowls, scattered with the remaining spring onions and with the runny boiled eggs on top and chilli sauce on the side.

5 eggs

3 tablespoons oil (sesame is best)

3 cloves of garlic

500g beef mince

1 teaspoon ginger purée

6 spring onions

2 tablespoons soy sauce

2 tablespoons teriyaki sauce

500g pre-cooked microwaveable basmati rice (2 packets)

2 pak choi

Chicken Shawarma Burgers

SERVES: 4 • TIME: 40 MINUTES

I often make these sloppy, juicy, flavour-packed shawarma burgers when I've got people coming over. They're a real crowd pleaser. Not too spicy for the kids and a delicious treat for adults. I serve the shawarma in a big bowl with some slaw and a stack of brioche buns. You'll always find people huddled around the meat scooping out extra.

1. Finely chop the garlic and put it into a bowl with the chicken, 3 tablespoons of Greek yoghurt, the cumin, smoked paprika, Cajun seasoning, and plenty of salt and pepper. Mix well. Cover and place in the fridge to marinate for a few hours or overnight.

2. When ready to cook, put the chicken into the air fryer and cook on 200°C for 10–12 minutes.

3. While the chicken is cooking, make a salad for the burgers. Chop the tomato, red onion, parsley and half the chillies and put them into a bowl with the lemon juice and the remaining tablespoons of Greek yoghurt.

4. Toast your burger buns, ready to serve.

5. Remove the chicken from the air fryer and put it on a chopping board. Chop, using a sharp knife. Spread a tablespoon of mayonnaise on each bun, then add some chicken to each one, with some salad mix on top, and top with some pickled onions and the rest of the chillies.

3 cloves of garlic

500g boneless chicken thighs

7 tablespoons Greek yoghurt

1 teaspoon ground cumin

1 teaspoon smoked paprika

1 teaspoon Cajun seasoning

salt and pepper

1 tomato

1 red onion

small handful of parsley, chopped

2 tablespoons pickled chillies

juice of 1 lemon

4 brioche burger buns

4 tablespoons of mayonnaise

shop-bought pickled pink onions, or regular pickled onions

Balsamic Beef Bourguignon

SERVES: 4 • TIME: 45 MINUTES

The mother of all stews, beef Bourguignon. I love adding extra balsamic to give it a sweet kick, and cooking it really slowly so the beef melts in your mouth. The perfect cosy midweek meal.

1. Chop the bacon, onion, carrots and 2 cloves of garlic. Put the bacon into a large soup pan or casserole dish with a couple of tablespoons of olive oil and fry until crispy. Remove the bacon from the pan and set aside on a plate, then add the beef pieces and fry them in the same pan for a few minutes on both sides, until they start to turn golden.

2. Remove the beef and put it on the plate with the bacon. Add the chopped onion, carrots and garlic to the pan, then add the balsamic vinegar and cook until the veg are soft. Put your meat back in, then sprinkle the flour over everything and mix well.

3. Add the tomato purée and cook for 2 minutes, stirring well. Pour in the wine (if using) and bring to the boil. Boil for 2 minutes then add the stock, bay leaf, and season with plenty of salt and pepper. Chop the thyme leaves and add to the pan, stir, then put a lid on and cook on a low heat for 2 hours.

4. When the cooking time is nearly up, slice the mushrooms and chop the remaining clove of garlic. Fry the mushrooms and garlic in a frying pan with butter until well cooked.

5. Remove the lid of the soup pan and stir in the mushrooms.

6. Serve with mashed potato and warm crusty bread with plenty of butter!

6 rashers of smoked bacon

1 onion

2 carrots

3 cloves of garlic

olive oil

500g lean beef pieces

2 tablespoons balsamic vinegar

2 tablespoons plain flour

1 tablespoon tomato purée

250ml full-bodied red wine (optional)

500ml beef stock

1 bay leaf

salt and pepper

a handful of fresh thyme

250g button mushrooms

1 tablespoon butter

Index